Animals HIDDEN in the DESERT

Jessica Rusick

PEBBLE
a capstone imprint

Published by Capstone Press, an imprint of Capstone
1710 Roe Crest Drive
North Mankato, Minnesota 56003
capstonepub.com

Library of Congress Cataloging-in-Publication Data is available on the Library of Congress website.
ISBN: 9781666315509 (hardcover)
ISBN: 9781666318029 (paperback)
ISBN: 9781666315516 (ebook PDF)

Summary: Some desert creatures are masters of disguise! They use camouflage and cover to outsmart predators or sneak up on prey. Some desert animals blend in with rocks, sand, and more. Others burrow beneath the ground or hide in shrubs. Can you spot the creatures hidden in the desert?

Image Credits
iStockphoto: Gerald Corsi, 30, 32 (middle), JanJBrand, 15, jnnault, 16, 32 (bottom), Michael Valdez, 26, pabst_ell, 25, SoopySue, 23; Shutterstock: Alexander Wong, 11, Chantelle Bosch, 27, 29, Charles T. Peden, 3 (top), 17, 18, Dan Olsen, 3 (bottom middle), 28, Doyne and Margaret Loyd, 3 (bottom left), 7, Dr Ajay Kumar Singh, 24, Foto 4440, 9, 10, 31 (middle), HeavilyMeditated, 8, JayPierstorff, 12, 31 (top), Mark_Kostich, 3 (bottom right), 20, NOWAK LUKASZ, Cover, Owen65, 21, Paul Vinten, 19, Pixelheld, 13, Stu Porter, 1, 14, 31 (bottom), Uwe Bergwitz, 5, 22, 32 (top), Voodison328, 6

Design Elements
Mighty Media, Inc.

Editorial and Design Credits
Editor: Rebecca Felix, Mighty Media; Designer: Aruna Rangarajan, Mighty Media

Printed and bound in the USA. 4608

HIDDEN IN THE
DESERT

Some desert creatures are masters of disguise! They use camouflage and cover to outsmart predators or sneak up on prey. Some desert animals blend in with rocks, sand, and more. Others burrow beneath the ground or hide in shrubs. Can you spot the creatures hidden in the desert?

First, try to spot the animal hidden in the desert.
WHAT DO YOU THINK IT IS?

Turn the page to reveal the animal and learn more about it.
DID YOU GUESS RIGHT?

This big-eyed bird spends most of its time on the ground. What is it?

Turn and see!

IT'S A **BURROWING OWL!**

Burrowing owls nest underground. In deserts, they live in burrows left behind by other animals.

This speedy hopper has long ears and legs. What is it?

Turn and see!

IT'S A **BLACK-TAILED JACKRABBIT!**

Black-tailed jackrabbits can jump long distances to escape predators. Jackrabbits can also run fast. They can reach 40 miles (64 kilometers) per hour!

This armored mammal is great at digging. What is it?

Turn and see!

IT'S AN **ARMADILLO!**

Armadillos use their long claws to dig for bugs to eat. Armadillos also dig burrows. Burrows protect armadillos from predators.

This large lizard moves slowly. What is it?

Turn and see!

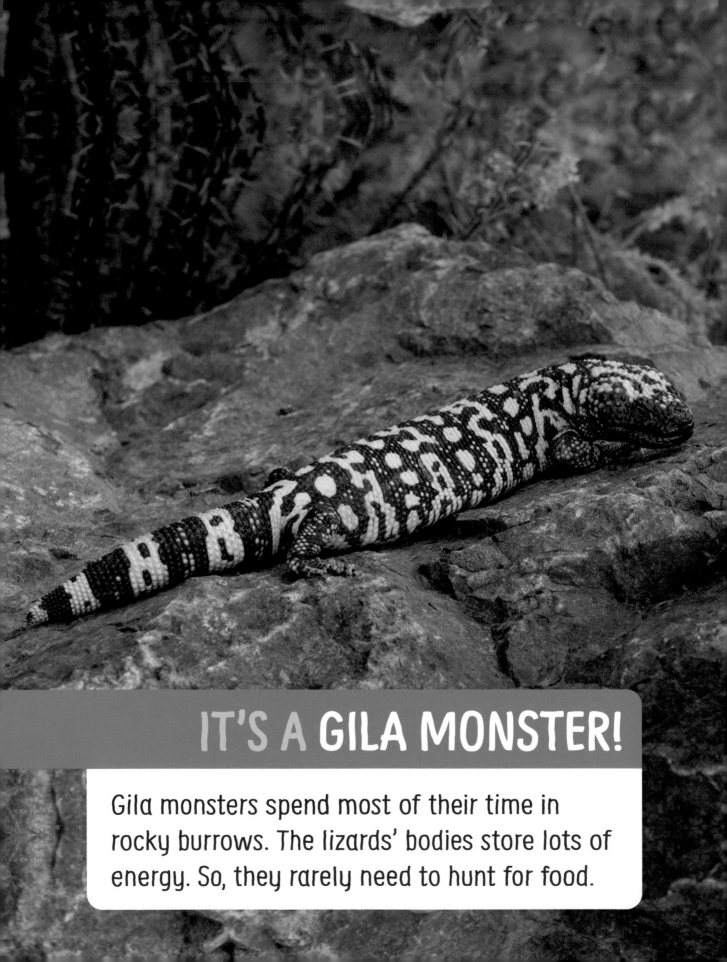

IT'S A GILA MONSTER!

Gila monsters spend most of their time in rocky burrows. The lizards' bodies store lots of energy. So, they rarely need to hunt for food.

This reptile can change color. What is it?

Turn and see!

IT'S A CHAMELEON!

A chameleon has special skin cells. They allow it to change color and pattern. A chameleon's appearance can change due to temperature, sunlight, or the animal's mood!

This hooved creature lives in rocky desert mountains. What is it?

Turn and see!

IT'S A NUBIAN IBEX!

Nubian ibex grip cliffs with their sharp hooves. Ibex also jump up mountain sides. They can jump more than 6 feet (1.8 meters) high!

This tiny mammal has light brown fur. What is it?

Turn and see!

IT'S A ROUND-TAILED GROUND SQUIRREL!

Round-tailed ground squirrels dig burrows. The burrows shade squirrels from the sun. When it is cool, the squirrels leave to find food. They eat cactus flowers, grasses, and more.

This scaly reptile has two tiny horns. What is it?

Turn and see!

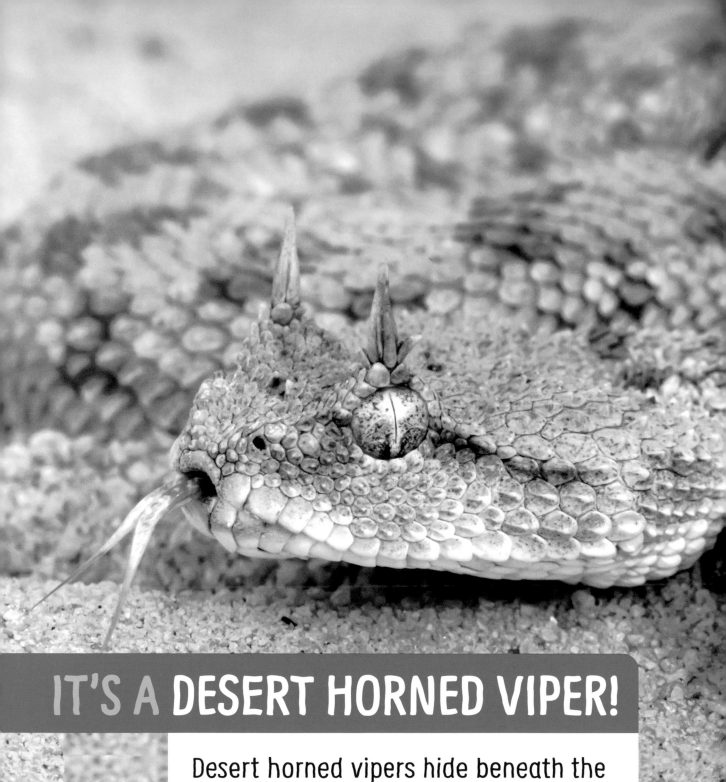

IT'S A DESERT HORNED VIPER!

Desert horned vipers hide beneath the sand. This makes them hard for prey to see. When prey gets close, the viper strikes! It bites with sharp fangs.

This desert dweller is covered in spines. What is it?

Turn and see!

IT'S A **THORNY DEVIL!**

A thorny devil's spines help it defend against predators. Thorny devils mainly eat ants. They can eat up to 2,500 ants in one meal!

This desert bird is most active at night. What is it?

Turn and see!

IT'S AN **EGYPTIAN NIGHTJAR!**

Egyptian nightjars sleep during the day. They rest beneath plants to stay hidden from predators. At night, the birds hunt for bugs.

This doglike mammal has pointed ears. What is it?

Turn and see!

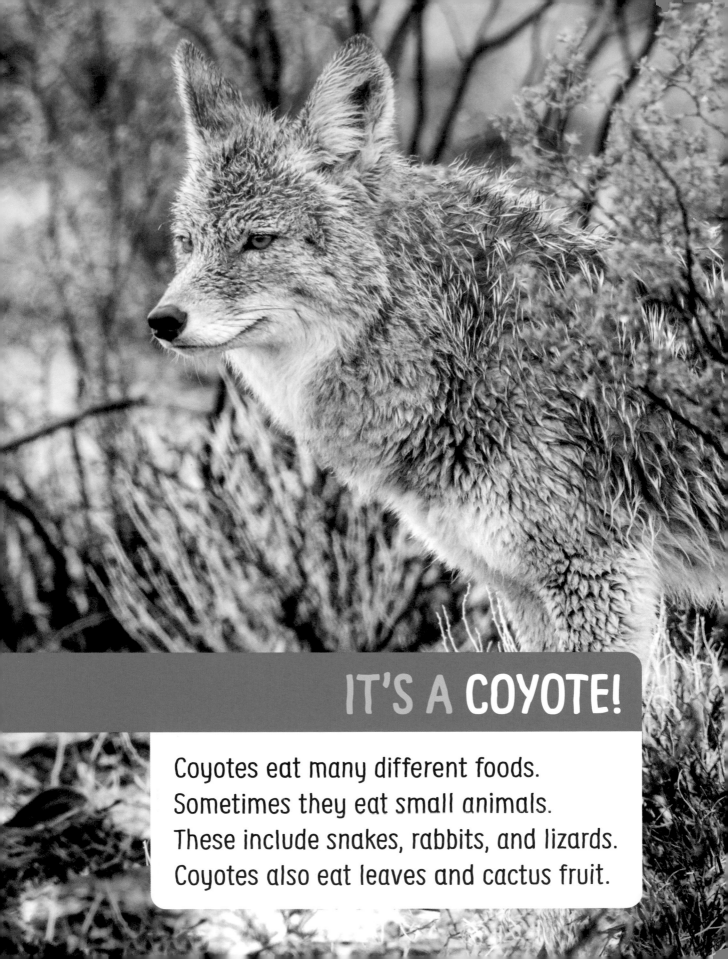

IT'S A COYOTE!

Coyotes eat many different foods.
Sometimes they eat small animals.
These include snakes, rabbits, and lizards.
Coyotes also eat leaves and cactus fruit.

This crawly creature has many eyes and legs. What is it?

Turn and see!

IT'S A SIX-EYED SAND SPIDER!

Six-eyed sand spiders hide under the sand. They wait to attack prey. These spiders are among the deadliest on Earth. They kill prey with strong venom.

This slithering snake has sand-colored scales. What is it?

Turn and see!

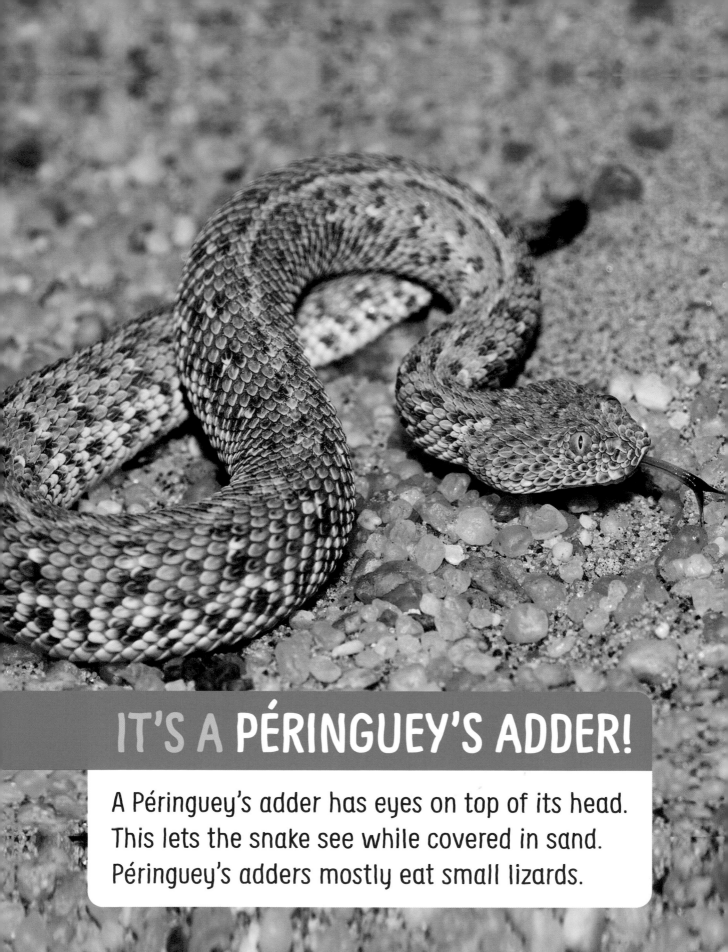

IT'S A PÉRINGUEY'S ADDER!

A Péringuey's adder has eyes on top of its head. This lets the snake see while covered in sand. Péringuey's adders mostly eat small lizards.

FUN FACTS

Gila monsters only need to eat a few meals per year to survive.

An armadillo burrow can be up to 15 feet (4.5 m) long.

A chameleon has one of the fastest moving tongues of any animal.

A thorny devil's spines are made from the same material as human fingernails.

Péringuey's adders move fast. They can slither at 18 miles (29 km) per hour!

Male Nubian ibex have long, curved horns.